Pen It
The People's Accounts, Emotions, and
Thoughts of 2020

Volume II

Publications

Treasures from the King

Finding Your Me

A Child's Tenth

When I Grow (Blow) Up

Shaping My Path

Toilet Treats

Writing Your Story

The 52 Experience

Pen It, Volume I

The Recipe Reminder

.........Pen It
Volume II
Compiled by Pam Ryans

DEDICATION

Writing is an outlet. It is a place to house emotions and thoughts. It's is a place to share actual accounts and create imaginary events. Fortunately, and unfortunately, 2020 wrote a message on the memories of many lives for years to come.

Therefore, this volume is dedicated to the lives with memories etched in their hearts and minds that can never be erased. Additionally, this volume is dedicated to each author who shared their memories in "Pen It, Volume I."

—

CONTENTS

—

INTRODUCTION

There are millions of reported deaths and counted births. We've faced church, businesses, and school closings. The hearts, minds, and lives of the people are impacted by triumph and tragedy, and we continue by GOD's grace. Each soul has its own feeling, and each mind has its own perception. "Pen It" Volume One captures the raw emotions and thoughts of real-time accounts.

January 1, 2020, began on a Wednesday at midnight. For many, it started with a celebration filled with laugher and high hopes for a prosperous year. Well, that's the perspective of the United States of America. Yet across the globe, January 1, 2020, was just an ordinary day.

Pen It Volume II continues the emotions and thoughts of those who lost loved ones, including themselves. In the midst of a world crisis, the real tragedy is when self feels helpless and hopeless. Many felt hopeless and many still feel helpless with the job situations, economical crisis, even more illness and death, and seemingly no relief in sight.

On the other hand, others see something other than hopeless and helpless. They see hopeful and helpful. They have created an avenue to a better way of thinking. And, once we begin to think differently, we can create a different day.

—

Pen It

The People's Accounts, Emotions, and
Thoughts of 2020

Volume II

A TESTIMOMY OF LOVE
-Tony O. Harris Brooks-

ABC, one, two, three, Lord not me, but thee.

XYZ, four, five six the world can leave me alone. My Lord, my God is upon his throne.
The prince of the air is making the strong blow.

Gale force winds of lies, treachery, and deceit rages against mine soul. If truth be lies, and lies be truth?
Where is my sanity?
Is what it is, really what it is?

There is something about the spiritual realm that turns this world around. There are forces aligning themselves for war.

A battle that will last throughout the ages.
Let God only be truth.
This earth shall soon pass away.
With all these troubles and woes that are dire to my soul.

As I write this, COVID-19 is ravaging around the world.
It has killed over one half a million people, and the numbers are still climbing.

The Biden/Harris ticket won the Presidential 2020 election.
Donald J. Trump exclaims, "The election was stolen, I won by a lot."

His trumpery has fooled many in the nation.
Now all the skeletons are coming out the closet.
Racist, neo-nazies and white supremacists have attacked the Capital. Believing themselves patriots and fighting for Trump's presidential honor.

If truth be lies and lies be truth, we all are damn to hell.
President Joseph R. Biden really has his work cut out for him.
Scientists have done what has never ever been done before.
All hands-on deck to rid our world of the COVID-19 virus,
Now the virus DNA variants have the ability to infect more fiercely.

Our scientists say, "The vaccines are safe. We have the knowledge.
The way we made the vaccines can be readjusted as necessary to fight COVID-19." Those highly politicized vaccines offer hope and visions of normalcy.

Normalcy?
What is that?
We return to what?
Do we return to what made America great, again?
Where people are hated and killed for the color of their skin?
When the black intelligence is mocked and counted as naught?
By God, by laws all men are created equal.
Yet the status quo dictates evils designed to keep us underfoot.

ABC, one, two, three,
Oh Lord not me, but thee.
XYZ, four, five six
God is in the mix.
I have to examine the me that no one really see.
Because I see my flaws and my imperfections.
I understand my beauty is not for the world,
But for thee.

My self-worth is more than how the world judges my status quo. Praise you God for coming to my rescue.

You gave me a heart of flesh when my love turned stone cold. You've sheltered me and loved me and taught me just how to be loved. No matter what is going on in the world as it spins from day to night,
I see the troubles and woes tearing at my very existence.
If you are white you right, red, yellow, black, and brown stay down.
I experience all the hurts and pains of a black women.
I'm not a weak someone to be pitied, nor to be taken lightly.
This world brings many challenges as I walk through.
Its flag of entitlement, white supremacy, and voter suppression,
Waves boldly upon the breeze as it chokes out the very air I breathe.

Is not the world my oyster?
What's in it for me?
My mind sees a place where I am unencumbered by this world.
Its begging pleads and wants to have sucked a hole in my
chest. No! I shall not let it rip out my heart of flesh.
This diseased world shall not be my tomb.

Once I tried to kill myself.
Overwhelming fears of peer pressures, and what others
expected of me. Devoured my mind and my soul.
Ha ha ha!

I can laugh now.
I smile inside myself.
Your grace showed up and saved my life.
Sure, I knew those pills and alcohol would work their magic.
After all, no one at home to intervene.
I was so disappointed to awake to the foul smell of vomit
waste, saturating my pillows and sheets with all my insides
turned out. You said, "Not yet, the adventure has only begun.

Wow what an adventure, since I tried to kill myself.
I was young then and now a seasoned citizen.
So many childhood dreams left in the past have reawakened.
New life has rejuvenated my soul.
Lord, you showed me that I mattered.
Wherever I've been
Whatever I've done.

I desire to make a difference because I am my brother's
keeper.

The world outside is cold.
People take kindness for weakness.
I am mocked and played the fool.
How foolish does the world think I am?
I've given it too much of me.
Enough is enough!
I'm living my best life as; I walk away from this wasteland.
This world promises much and gives very little.

Well Lord, I thank you that I can sit at home during this
COVID-19 season.

Don't have to work from sun up until sun down slaving with the woes of the world, Its scheming and cheating ways to disenfranchise and devalue me.
Don't have to stand there and watch evil sneer in my face.
Nope, don't have to give the world nothing of me.
Not that I'm selfish, but I come first.
It's time to put my energies into my dreams.
Thank you for giving me the strength to walk away from strife.
You promised and gave me a down-to-earth love.
And best of all, he humbles himself before you.
Yes, you've given me the ability to trust and believe in the majesty of you.

Lord your love has kept me throughout the years,
Long before Covid-19 ever became one of my fears.
And you've given me the courage to believe in faith's infinity.
Though I may know what my future hold,
Nor what tomorrow may bring.
I know that little 'ole insignificant me, matter.
During this Covid-19 season, you are polishing and molding me. Revitalizing the layers of tarnish that has marred my beauty
I'm covered in peace as you heal mind and soul,
As you sculpture me into a marvelous work of art.
I can go about my business with the urgency of you.

There is something about the spiritual realm that spins into reality. If truth be lies, and lies be truth?
Is what it is, really what it is?
ABC, one, two three,

Oh Lord not me, but thee. XYZ, four, five, six,
My Lord, my God is the fix. You are Alpha and Omega, The Beginning and the End, And I love you.

It's Time
-Romi Darling-

2020 you came for me so vigorously that I had to fight back with power!

I had to conjure my power in order to believe what God told me in 2019.

Because in 2019, God said, "It's Time."

2020 started with great intentions with goals that were set and had to be achieved. Coming into the year, I was more focused than I had ever been. I was a 33-year-old college student with so much to prove to myself; because of how my life was set up.

In a time where I was so focused, a curved ball (Covid-19) was thrown, coming in at a hot 90 mph, "Strike!" I'm like DAMN! Covid sat the world down, but the world couldn't handle it. Hell, for a minute, I didn't think I could, but I remember what God said, "it's time." Son, I had to adjust my mentality. I began to silence the noise. I began to silence the media because it was becoming too loud, as if it was a child speaking out of turn. Remembering God's voice "Ball," I'm still in the game.

Strike two came a little faster and with some power behind it. My uncle's death came as a total shock to my family. And it shocked me to my core because of the space that my uncle and I were in. We hadn't really spoken in a while, but God allowed us to make peace one week before his death. In his death, I realized the strength I was blessed with. This strength is not only for myself but for the people I love.

Foul! Down the third-base line still in the game! I was forced into being homeless because I chose to stand for what was right. We had been living in a material place that we needed to lay our heads, to cleanse our bodies, to feed our souls, and to enjoy one another. But that was short-lived due to the neglect by the owner.

While sleeping on my best friend's floor, I had choices to make. First, do I allow this to hurt me and keep me from God's promise? Or secondly, do I remember God's promise and keep working towards the destination while staying present throughout the journey and witness the works of our God?

Two strikes, one ball, and a foul, we are still in the game! While Covid-19 is still on the rise, so is God. I was still able to achieve so many small goals that I set for this year, and with faith, my mother and my son, along with so many other earth angels, I'm still standing because I listened to the promise God said to me.

We are down to the wire! It's just me and the pitcher (distractions). POW, it goes deep, and it's out of there! Homerun! I was headed on a business trip and got the phone call that changed the game, A HOME, PEACE, and FREEDOM.

I thank God daily for the many blessings that were given to me by Him. I know that Covid-19 is real, but I also know God is real and more powerful than any distraction, virus, and disease in this world. Covid took a lot from us all, but it also gave us some powerful angels to watch over us and guide us to that promise.

Don't get distracted with fear or negative thoughts. Remember God said It's time.

May God bless us all with light and love.

My heart goes out to everyone who has lost a loved one to this terrible virus and the ones who have overcome the virus.

Peace and Love to you all.

Romi

Joy
-Dr. Dionne Edison-

LORD, good morning. Wow, the birds are really singing this morning. Their winged chorus of praise for this day blots out the drumbeat of dread that comes with daily COVID-19 updates. I'm reminded just as YOU meet their needs YOU also meet mine.

Thank YOU for every day. I'm excited to see what each day has in store. I know the plans YOU have for me are good and better than any I could imagine for myself. I trust YOU to guide me as I place everything before YOU. (Jeremiah 29:11, Proverbs 3:5-6) These days Lord, there is a weight on my heart in the midst of my praise not so much for myself as for others. Often, I bemoan this worldwide valley pandemic experience as each day brings more pain and heartache. Yet, in the midst of everything, there is JOY. I am grateful.

COVID-19 has exposed many ways that money, power and influence corrupt business, politics, and even faith-based communities. So many people lost their jobs. Businesses permanently shuttered doors. Schools closed. Hospitals had to turn away patients. Health providers, first responders, front liners had to choose between work and family while not receiving a COVID-19 exemption from exhaustion, illness or death.

People quit jobs to become care providers for children, parents or other relatives. Women, minorities, the elderly, and others were further marginalized. Those experiencing disproportionate disparities have born the brunt of the economic losses and setbacks. Morgues used refrigerated trucks to hold the massive overflow of bodies as families await the opportunity to say their final goodbyes. This does not begin to depict the entirety of a world in crisis. The world keeps turning on a shifting axis. And yes, LORD there is still JOY.

There is JOY that comes with the realization that not only am I not alone, but I am not in charge. YOU are. For every trial there is triumph. For every tear there are rays of sunshine. For every dreadful thumping drumbeat of the heart there is a staccato flutter of ecstasy. Somebody was revived today. Someone was healed. Someone made peace. Someone gave today all that they had. Someone received today a gift unexpected. Someone walked, a baby or veteran taking first steps. New birth or rebirth there is much more for which to be glad. Yes, LORD, even for which to have JOY.

There they are LORD, the birds. They are really putting on a concert. Birds, the currency of mercy, were sacrificed. Birds, the food for wanderers, fed the whiners freed from 400 years of slavery. A bird, the messenger of good news, acknowledged a SON in whom THE FATHER is well pleased. I slow down and pay attention as I watch the birds.

My journey with YOU, LORD, is amazing. Birds cannot sing my song of praise. No one can tell my story. So, in the midst of this COVID-19 pandemic, I look to YOU. I, too, sing for YOU. I am convinced death, life, angels, principalities, powers, things present, things to come, highs, lows, or any man/creature, cannot separate me from YOUR love. (Romans 8:38-39) That gives me peace beyond all understanding and unspeakable JOY.

LORD, I'm grateful. I Thank YOU. In JESUS' name I Joyfully pray. AMEN.

The Two Pandemics
-Sheila D. Green-

If you take a close look at what is happening in our society; it's apparent that there are 2 types of pandemics going on; one is COVID-19 and the other one is racism and hatred. Both pandemics are disproportionately affecting African Americans, particularly African American men. Right now, we are living through a period of unprecedented racial hatred. We have to face the harsh reality that millions of us are being treated differently because of the color of our skin.

These are definitely uncertain times, and the two pandemics are having a major impact on our mental health.
So, with all this uncertainty in the air as people, we feel the need to do something, fix something or prevent something from happening.

Wanting to do something, doing something and not knowing what to do; causes a tremendous amount of stress and anxiety in our lives. And it's during these times, that caring for yourself matters the most.

The pandemic has changed how we work, learn, and play. Social distancing guidelines have led us to a more virtual reality, both professionally and personally. So, it no surprise that the magnitude of these changes have triggered a wave of mental health issues. There has been in an increase in addictions, depression and social isolation. And because our younger people are social creatures, they appear to be impacted the most.

In spite of all that's going on, yourself care is of the uttermost importance. Here are some suggestions on how to practice self care during a crisis:

•Take care of your body by staying active, limiting your intake of sugars and processed foods and be sure to get plenty of sleep.

•It's important to stay socially connected. It's a good idea to communicate with one person outside of your home each day. And do not forget to check on those family members and friends who live alone and may be feeling isolated during this time.

•Make an effort to keep work and living space free of clutter. Clutter and disorganization cause stress and interferes with your ability to relax mentally and physically.

•Be mindful of your social media consumption. Repeatedly watching or reading negative stories can increase feelings of stress and anxiety.

•Prayer! The number of deaths and infections caused by COVID-19 as well as the fight against systematic racism has created and spread a lot of fear. One of the best antidotes for fear is prayer. Make prayer a part of your daily routine. It will provide peace and decrease your overall stress levels.

•Therapy! During times such as these, we may be experiencing more stress, worry and anxiety as usual. If these emotions persist or worsen counseling or therapy may be needed. Those with pre-existing mental health conditions should continue with treatment.

•Having an attitude of gratitude takes the focus off what is going on around you helps you to appreciate all the good things that are a part of your life.

•And last but not least, find something to do each day that makes you happy. Use, your imagination, be good to yourself and kinds to others.

I would be remiss if I didn't address the negative impact that the pandemic has had on our relationships. Couples have been isolating at home for more than a year, trying to stay safe and keep loved ones safe. But after prolonged periods of continually being together in close quarters, all the coziness can become overwhelming. How do you take care of your relationship when everything else around you is spinning out of control? Here are four tips that I recommend to help couples rekindle the flame.

#1: Maintain a Self Care Routine

The first thing you want to do is take care of yourself. Get up and show up for yourself each day. Set up and maintain some sort of routine. It might not be a bad idea to put on something other than pajamas during the day. Be sure you get enough sleep and take breaks when needed. Stay active and eat nutritious foods. Set boundaries and find one thing to do each day that you enjoy. When you take better care of you, you are able to appreciate and enjoy those around you.

#2: Put Limitations on Your Work Day

For couples who are working from home it will help to set boundaries between work hours and the time you spend together. Try to keep personal and professional work spaces separate. If possible, have separate work spaces and be intentional about the time you spend together. Limit your interactions during the day so you can look forward to spending time together at the end of your day.

#3: Don't Skip The Romance!

You should check in with your partner regularly. Even if you know your partner extremely well, we are all experiencing something that we've never experienced before.
Finding time to become physically intimate can become increasingly difficult under the umbrella of all this chaos. This is time where flexibility and creativity are key.
Get up early or go to bed late in order to find that quiet time that you need together.
Order flowers or leave love notes where each of you can find them.
Send a steamy text message during the middle of the day suggesting what you would like to do that night. Remember intimacy is a way for the two of you to stay connected.

The pandemic won't last forever. Focusing on your relationship and making yourself a priority can leave couples better off once this pandemic is over and things return to normal.

These are uncertain times and it's ok to make up the rules as you go; as long as you consider and maintain the respect and integrity that you have for yourselves and for each other.

#4 Find Your Joy
And last but not least, find something to do each day that makes you happy! Find something to engage in that relaxes you, recharges you, rejuvenates you and brings you joy. Use your imagination. Practice being good to yourself and don't forget to be kind to others.

I'm going let you in on a little secret; if you can practice self care during a crisis then you can practice self care during any season. Self care is not selfish. A healthier, happier you will help you to enjoy and take care of those around you. Remember, self care is for everyone and everyone should be practicing self care!

As restrictions are being lifted and there are vaccinations in place; I'm sure we all are thankful for making it to this point, hopeful for the healing and restoration of our nation and prayerful for equality and justice for all; regardless of race, creed or religion.

God Wants to Fill the Empty Places
-Emma Hall-

2020 into 2021 have and shall be the promotion to the progress of God's faithfulness unto me. What has happened to me in 2020 has actually only served to advance, prepare, mature, and give me renewed strength and new insight into 2021. It renewed and caused my trust and faith to be deepened. I experienced a new hunger for God, His Word, and His heart's desire for me. I was reignited like never before. We have a God who listens to our prayers and answers them according to His perfect will.

In a nutshell, I'm a better person. What the enemy meant for evil to destroy me, uproot my love, faith, and peace in my God, elevated me to leap into His arms to be embraced, have one-on-one, face-to-face conversations with Him without distractions and interruptions. I ran to the ROCK of my salvation. I'm running now. He granted me the privilege, for Christ's, sake not only to believe in, adhere to, rely on, and trust Him but also to suffer on His behalf. Selah. God's mercy, grace, love, and faithfulness brought me and kept me through it all. If it were not for God, I would have lost my sanity (mind). 2020 was one of the most blessed years of my life. My faith, love, and trust in the Lord were really tested.

During this time, I experienced many challenges that uprooted things and changed my perspective about life. But I made it through and continuing with sanity in Christ Jesus. I made an intentional decision to sit at the feet of Jesus to be taught, strengthened, find love, protection, peace, and joy in the Holy Spirit. He is the Spirit of Truth who instructed and guided me through it all.

I did more listening than talking. The battle had begun in my mind to bring doubt and unbelief that my God wasn't enough. I had to feed myself on the supernatural food of God's Word for my weapon against my adversary. My mental, emotional and thought life. I had to bring in alignment according to

God's Word. I had to overcome many different changes, challenges, and obstacles, but not alone. He was there all the time to comfort me, wipe my tears away, and help me understand the struggles are real. He said that I Am more real than all. I Am your God. The true, real, and living God that has been your Provider all of your life. He showed His faithfulness.

There was a time I didn't know where food or monies to pay bills was coming from. My God supplies all my need according to His glory in Christ Jesus. Trust God! He is faithful and true to all His promises and Word. I know that the power of God's Holy Spirit was working in me and through me to empower me with wisdom, knowledge, revelation, and understanding. In my weakness, He is made strong. Amen. Jesus is our only answer for the world today. I keep falling more and more in LOVE WITH HIM. He's the KEEPER and BISHOP of my entire being.

Many became hopeless, faithless, lost their joy, peace, etc., but I, friend, ground myself in the Word of God, prayer, and positive thinking. I speak God's Word to my mountains, obstacles, situations, circumstances, finances, etc. He said we're to tell them what His Word says about them. They have to move out of our way. (Matt. 17:20). Discouragement and hopelessness only come when we see our problems through our human eyes rather than focusing on His perspectives. Holy Spirit reminded me times after times of the VICTORIES that were already mine. In the midst of it all, maturity, faith, trust, was elevated to higher heights in Him. My roots are growing deeper and deeper in God's love. I'm sitting in another place in Jesus. I found out that my measure of faith is in Him. He empowered me and is ever-increasing my faith.

Be encourage we have a God that knows, feels, and has been through all we are going through. He will never forsake you nor leave you alone in these uncertain, unpredictable times.

God's lockdown (lock-in) was definitely a for me to get focused and get my life in order. And I give Him all the glory for the thing He has done in me, bringing me back in focus. It's all about His Love for His people.

Therefore, never lose heart, faith, or your joy while going through, instead renew your mind with the Word of God. (Phil.4:8, Rom.12:2). We must keep the faith in His divine Power, knowing our God is more than able to take us through the shadow of death. These times are just a shadow. Our God is greater than them all. He's the Great I Am That I Am, the Creator, Almighty God, our Refuge, Hiding Place, Provider, Might God, Savior, and Healer. Whatsoever we need Him to be, He already is. He's in our past, present, and future. He has gone on before us to prepare a place for us.

GOD wants to fill the empty places in our lives. (Psalm 103:5). When we feel empty and unloved, we can turn to God for both love and filling. In truth, we're promised the HOPE that we will not be disappointed. (Romans 5:5). God has given us the Holy Spirit to fill our innermost being, hearts, minds, emptiness, souls with all of who He is. He invites us to open our mouths so He can fill them. (Psalm 81:10)

Today you may be in need. Is it possible that you have some empty areas in your life right now? Maybe there are aches, pains, hurts, or disappointments within your soul that no one knows about but the Lord. Be encouraged that our Lord is able to do exceedingly, supernaturally, abundantly above all we can ask, think, or imagine because of His power that's at work in us. He's able to abundantly fill every empty place with His love and meet our every need. Of course, He wants to fill us up to overflow. The Lord satisfies the thirsty and fills the hunger within us with good things, whether an actual thirst or hunger or an emotional thirst or hunger or spiritual hunger. Our Lord God is able to meet our needs (Psalm 107: 9, Philippians 4:19). When we come into a personal relationship with Jesus, we can enjoy every benefit of being His. Ephesians 5:18 tells us not to be drunk with wine but filled with the Spirit of God. All this comes when we totally and completely surrender and commit to God. When we give everything to God, we get out of the way.

I bless you in Jesus' Name. Embrace every promise and all benefits given to you by your Father, God.

Fetching, Feeding, and Fixing
-Rev. Dr. B. Nelson Little-

Pastor Little's favorited scripture is Romans 8:28 "We know all things work together for our good."

Fetching: I am not ashamed (Romans 1:16)

Feeding: There is none righteous, not one (Romans 3:10)

All, have sinned and fallen short of His Glory (Romans 3:23)

For the wages of sin is death (Romans 6:23)

Fixing: The gift of God is eternal life in Christ (Romans 6:23)

But God demonstrates his own love for us in this: While we were still sinners, Christ died for us (Romans 5:8)

If you declare with your mouth, "Jesus is Lord," and believe in your heart that God raised him from the dead, you will be saved. For it is with your heart that you believe and are justified, and it is with your mouth that you profess your faith and are saved. for, "Everyone who calls on the name of the Lord will be saved Romans 10:9-10;13)

Vantage Point
- Antoinette Lott-

A position which gives you an advantage or clear view!
2020 came in with a powerful word "The wait is over! "As I
look back on that sermon, I can't help but dig a bit deeper into
its message. I am sure a lot of speakers are doing the same.
When we hear a powerful word, we tend to apply it to our lives
for where we are at that moment. However, we overlook where
God is trying to take us. Yet once reality hits and the word
begins to unfold, and we come to embrace what the message
was truly trying to convey, we are left in awe! Every single
person on this earth has had a different experience when
Covid -19 surfaced. Same monster, yet entirely different
impact. It became challenging to discuss the topic due to the
diversity of thoughts, so many of us chose to isolate ourselves
and our thoughts. Trying to understand exactly what was
happening was a challenge. So many conflicting stories and
nothing being clear and concise.

In the beginning, I tried to stay tuned in, but it quickly became
too heavy. All the reports caused so much confusion, so I chose
to unplug from the media and put my focus on God. My bible
tells me not to be conformed to the world but be transformed
by the renewing of my mind, so I did just that! Putting in the
energy to stay connected to the world was stressful, and it
changed nothing. However, embracing the Word had a major
impact on my life and those God placed in my path. The Word
allowed me to be strengthened when someone became weak. It
allowed me to pray for those in need. Keeping my eyes on God
and His Word brought about great change in me. All that time
at home alone gave me an opportunity to have some one-on-
one time with the Master.

Being home in isolation was very tough at times; the silence
was deafening. I never knew silence could be so loud. Not
being able to have a face-to-face conversation is something I
believe we have taken for granted in our society. Electronic

devices have eased in and taken the place of human contact and are now considered the new normal.

It also caused a distance in affection; we were and still are hesitant to embrace one another. We were forced to rely on our devices to express love and every other emotion. Love has been reduced to a heart emoji. Physical touch is essential for growth and healing, and social distancing has been catastrophic in more ways than one. There was a time in my life when allowing someone to hug me was exceedingly difficult, but as I grew older and closer to God, I learned to trust Him more, and putting my heart and emotions in his hands helped me to become more open to hugs. I would never have imagined that this would be something I would miss.

Being single is challenging enough, and this created an entirely new dimension of oneness. This new and sometimes unexplainable life has given me a new perspective on being single. I used to view it as some type of cruel and unusual punishment. Yes, that was my view; however, I refused to stay there, so I started this journey of preparedness. I prepared my mind so that I could have a healthy relationship. First with God, then with myself, which would ultimately lead to having a lifelong healthy marriage.

Hatred and racism have again become more accepted, and it has given the enemy an open avenue to kill, steal and destroy! Hate crimes increased because some took advantage of their so-called privilege. What was once sleeping was awakened! The covid monster caused other monsters to be exposed and wreak havoc on unsuspecting humans. We cried out for justice, yet there was no justice to be found! The symbol of justice was the monster, so we became fearful, cautious, and angry. Not realizing that this was a monster itself, the moment we gave in to fear and hatred created a monster within us that is hard to defeat. God did not give us a spirit of fear but of power, love, and a strong mind, yet we fell into the trap. The monster blocked our view of God. We became distracted and focused on killing the monster. The more we fought, the stronger the monster became. We were fighting a monster that fed off our anger, frustration, racism, indignation, isolation, fear, and every other negative emotion we produced.

Financially, it destroyed lives by taking jobs and forcing people from homes, as if we did not already have a big enough homeless population. However, in some instances, finances did not cease. It just became more stressful. Essential workers continued to go to work but at great risk to themselves as well as their families. Because somehow there were people that thought covid -19 was a joke or a hoax, and they continued to flood the retail stores by the thousands. They became offended when asked to respect the 6-ft no contact rule as if essential workers were expendable. Those with families had to be extra cautious and change the rules of engagement concerning their families. Imagine trying to explain to a toddler why they could not hug mommy or daddy as they were so accustomed to doing as soon as they arrived home. The psychological effects are unexplainable and, even more importantly, the long-term effects of this on our future generations. The loss of life has been so astounding that it seems like something out of a doom's day movie. There were so many dead bodies that alternative storage solutions were created. The part of this scenario that grips me is, life was reduced to a multitude of bodies with no storage!

2Chronicles7:14
If my people, which are called by my name, shall humble themselves, and pray, and seek my face, and turn from their wicked ways; then will I hear from heaven and will forgive their sin and will heal their land.

I believe absolutely everyone has become familiar with this scripture since Covid-19 surfaced. We have found many scriptures to try and explain the monster we had to face daily. Many have prayed prayers of healing, rebuke, and casting away, and yet the monster remained. God is the God of all things, and He reigns supreme. Imagine, for a moment, if He answered each prayer that was prayed since this monster appeared. Prayers are often prayed amiss, innocent, and heartfelt but amiss.

Looking at this verse, depending on who is teaching, we will get many different vantage points on what it means. None will ever understand what God fully intends because we are not all-seeing as he is. The word nourishes each of us differently because we a structured differently and therefore need something different. I can recall an eye-opening experience from basic training. We were all given the same meals, same proportions, at the same time daily. However, it affected each of us; differently. Some gained weight, and some lost. Yet, the result was consistent. We all became physically fit and ready for battle if the need arose.

The word of God works in the same manner. It does what is intended based on the needs of the reader. We fail to understand that when we read such an intense verse, we must be detailed in our reading and understanding. It begins with "IF "that tells me that all condition must be met by all of Gods people. What is the likely chance that every child of God knows this scripture and its conditions? That would take some absolute unity, but that is not likely due to race, creed, culture, and denomination. So, praying this scripture in hopes that God will heal our land from Covid -19 seems rather unobtainable, but God! He is able to do exceedingly and abundantly above anything we could ever ask or think!

Covid-19 put the faith of Christians on display for all the world to see. It was like a king or queen trying to avoid the media; it never works. The world was either taking their cues from Christians or waiting for an opportunity to destroy the faith we stated we had! It was and still is challenging for Pastors and preachers to keep the flock connected and encouraged. I have often asked while teaching a bible study or ministry group, "If your life was a billboard, what would it say or what would it look like?" Covid-19 has done that very thing by putting all Christians on display. Hoping to see us fall apart, break under pressure, and even see if we could still speak and live God's word. It leveled the playing field, in a sense, because God has been silent from the perspective of some. When God is silent, there is a lot of weeping and whaling, and life becomes stressful and overwhelming. As Christians, we have become accustomed to hearing from God through answered prayers and Rhema word. We were used to giving praise and honor through song and dance, listening to the preacher share what God said to them, going to the altar, and receiving prayer and anointing, gathering in fellowship with family, and seeing people face to face. Yes, the church is just a building, and yes, the true church is within every true believer, but when your world changes dramatically as it did, it is tough to adjust! Not being able to fellowship with people you love and are used to seeing on a regular is tough; I do not care who you are! As much as I enjoy my space, my peace, and my oneness, I also love people.

My most difficult challenge was delivering a sermon over the phone and not able to hear not one single Amen! Even though I have had to do this several times, it has not become comfortable. It has taught me to trust God even more and become more attentive to His voice. There is a song that says, "I need you; you need me we are all a part of God's body, stand with me agree with me I need you to survive!"

Every child born in 2020 and after was born into the wilderness, a world that lost the value of love. A world with fabricated emotions, a world without embraces or sincere affection. A world that hatred and racism are the daily normal. A world where the face of injustice is distorted. They have been born into a world consumed with electronic interaction. Now, human interaction is becoming a thing of the past. They have been born into a world where your true political stance is outweighed by the colors blue or red! They were born into a world where every church was closed while everything else was open!

Schools are open. Stores are open. Bars are open. Restaurants are open. Beauty shops are open. Barbershops are open. Gyms are open, And the stock market is open—every single brick and mortar building. OPEN! As a result, we get a generation of educated, well-dressed, alcoholic, overindulgent, well-groomed, possibly fit human beings that have no clue as to who God is. They will be emotionally distant because they have been deprived of human contact. They will be angry and confused due to the adult's lack of hope due to the state of mind. They will not know the true value of love because they will not know God.

So twenty years from now, when those children born in the wilderness become contributing members of society, and we wonder why our world is without order, and virtual reality is the only reality, we can look back and say, "I guess we should have opened the church." I understand the risk, and it is the same risk our essential workers take daily. It is the same risk that our teachers and children take daily. However, the church will not take the risk, even though we have firsthand knowledge of the one who took the biggest risk and sacrificed his life so that we could have eternal life. Thousands have crowded the streets to celebrate the win of their favorite team; their love and commitment to their team outweighed their fear. What kept them from sickness? It was not the excessive amount of alcohol that may have been in their system. It was not their complete disregard of the pandemic! It was Love! God had already decided from our birth when our lives would end. There is no such thing as premature when it comes to God. We may not be ready for the events of life, but God knows. I believe in the laws of physics that say for every action, there is a reaction! However, God knows our every action before we even think of it, so he knows every reaction.

Covid-19 has made me realize how little we trust God. No matter what it looks likes, God is still God. Even in his silence, he is still God! So, from whatever vantage point you have seen God!

Embrace God!

We Are Tired
-Cheyenne C. Nickleberry-

We are just so tired.
I've read so many stories and so many articles
Of how our world is trying to be torn to nothing but particles
I see the protests and hear the scream
I hear the scream of how Black America has a dream.
I hear the scream of our allied races standing up for us
I hear the scream of our allied races helping to make a fuss.
46-1 just had to say something stupid from the white house
But when we ran our mouth it had him hiding underground
like a mouse.
I see the riots and the protests
I know that we will no longer settle for less.
I see those who remain silent
Yet when there are issues with your rights you want to get
violent.
I notice how my people's back is against the wall
I see how we just want justice for those who suffered the fall.
The fall of oppression and racism
And now my brothers and sisters are rising with activism.
So yes, we are indeed tired
But now that we are finished with being tired, we are now
inspired.
Inspired to link with our brothers and sisters of another race
Inspired to link together and reach a higher place.

Do You Ever
-Sharonda Palmer-

Do you ever think of me the way I think of you?
Do you ever long for me the way I long for you?
Do you ever wish that we could talk and be together as before?
Do you ever wish that I would still love you more?

Do you ever wonder what our life was going to be like?
Do you ever think of me in the daylight?
Do you ever think of me when you dream?
Am I ever on your mind the way you stay in my scenes?
Do you ever think of me and want me by your side?
Do you ever think of me the way you are constantly on my mind?
Do you ever think of me every day like I think of you?
Did you ever really want me the way that I wanted you?

Do you ever wish that things for us will turn out great?
Or do you ever think that I was a huge mistake?
Do you ever feel like starting over with me again?
Or do you ever even think about wanting to be mine again?

Do you ever think that our love was just for show?
Or do you really think that our love was made for more?
Do you wish upon a star for us to be together at last?
Or do you wish that we had never met?

Do you ever think we could have been perfect for each other?
Or do you ever think that we were meant for another?
Do you ever think of me and long to feel my kiss?
Do you ever think of us and the life of love we possibly missed?
Do you ever think of us and the way we used to be?
Do you ever think of us and what we could have been truly?

I do think of us always and the love we shared so pure.
I do think of us and all the moments we held each other so true.
I do think of us and all the times we made each other laugh.
I do think of us and all the wonderful, exciting days we had.
I do think of us and all the days we only wanted to be close to each
other.
But now all I think of is if you will ever want me in your life again or
if you want another.

Please tell me that you think of me as much as I think of you. Please tell me that you love and need me as much as I still love and need you.

My Letter to God
-LaQueisha Price-

Dear God,

I am writing you to let you know 2020 was the year of opening up to you more. In 2021, I want to be closer to you, not just close, but I want you to dwell within me. I realize that I have underlying issues, but I do know that all things are possible with you. This journey has been a journey of peace, love, and prosperity. I can't forget about those who wronged me, those who made me feel less than, or those who didn't believe me or in me when I told them of the things you spoke in my life. I can't forget about the times when you were all I had, my Lord.

I'm writing to you with hopes and expectations that you would do all that you said you would do in my life, starting with 2021. I didn't get as much done as I would have liked in 2020, but I know that you will place the light within me to get it done with you within me. I'm not perfect, and I'm not trying to be perfect. You and I know I want to satisfy the great King.

I recognize myself as part of the kingdom, so I must take the good with the bad. I must smile when I'm sad. I love all that I have and remember the things that I had. I continue to work on building myself with the underlying issues that 2020 revealed. Loving self is also loving you.

I get up every morning thanking you for another day and praising your Name throughout the day. I may stumble but, I pick myself back up, learning not to wear my heart on my shoulder. I will continue to hold on to the fruitful spirits you have placed inside me; knowing, I have the greatest King on my side.

I love you like no other. I pray you continue to guide me in all the right directions. I pray you continue to cleanse my heart, mind, and soul daily from anything unrighteous; as I walk into

my greater knowing that I only have you. I just want you to
know how grateful and thankful I am

Your Daughter,
Laqueisha M. Price

Out of Sight, Out of Mind
-Reginald Prince-

Since I have been in prison, I have learned a lot of things. People seem to forget you; somehow, you become nothing. Many people support you at the beginning of your time, then you start to fade away. It's like out of sight, out of mind. Many make promises they know they can't keep. Some even lie to you about things in the streets. People at home don't know about the life we live behind bars, only what others hear in a song, not knowing it's really like hell. I'm sitting in my cell block all day and all night thinking as my future goals fade.

Out of Sight, Out of Mind

Many have wives and girlfriends who say they love you
only to discover that they are out with another dude.

Knowing how loved they are, the joy and times they shared,
giving all the faith and trust that one can while feeling like she
didn't even care.

Somehow the ones we love turn out to do us wrong,
and those who we took for granted turn out to be really strong.

So-called friends don't write or spend a dime.
Many so-called friends disappear - out of sight, out of mind.

Being in prison, many don't want too much out of you.
All they asked for is love and support, showing you truly care.

I have learned in prison no matter what situation you are in,
it always comes down to God first, family second.

I'm grateful for my beautiful wife, kids, and brother through this process. The thought of seeing them once again has been the only thing that has strengthened me through 2020 and this panoramic.

I hope that my story changes the taste of times. I hope your love, care, and support do not become out of sight out of mind.

Unfortunate Reality
-Kena Reshay

As our sons grow older,
we pray they escape the consequences of being black in
America.
We try our best to give them a good life and teach them to do
right.
But still, there's no escape of being black in America.
The day soon come that we'll have to explain.
The conversation.
Racism does exist.
The looks on their faces.
Africa.
Bought and sold.
Hated over what you can't control.
Just us.
No justice.
Our history.
Kings.
Queens.
Traditions.
Spiritual to Jah.
Free.
Captivity.
Door of no return.
Separated.
Torture.
400 years.
Shackles.
Tears.
Mental Fear.
Black bodies swinging.
Can't whistle.
Our experience.
Our reality.
Amerikkka.
Why can't they just be young forever?

Struggle
-Kamia Wardlaw-

(An Original Song)

It's a struggle (2x)

Ain't nobody there

Gotta hustle

It's a struggle

Verse:

Struggle is real

 kids are getting killed

Detroit's lost in time

some live on a dime

Take a walk in the park

run away from the dark

We don't know where to start

We or we're just so far apart

Yeah we falling apart

Gotta call on God

He's the only one

that can save us

But it's up to us

Give him all our trust (3x)

It's a struggle (2x)

Ain't nobody there

Gotta hustle

It's a struggle

2020 Pandemic, But Oh! For Grace
-Cece Washington-

Honestly, I didn't think I was doing very well. However, by His Grace, one year later, I get to tell about the benefits of Blessing the Lord at all times. Keeping His praise continually on my lips allowed no room for doubt and fear. Oh! Fear came upon me, and doubt certainly raised its head, but the practical application of the Word of God in those times truly sustained me. When I became weak, His Grace was sufficient in my weakness. Therefore, I can truly say of the Lord that He is my refuge and my strength. He was and continues to be a very present help in my times of need.

When I received the call from my daughter, I expected the call to be cheerful as always. She said, "I just feel bad momma, but I'm not afraid." I became so sad and mad at the devil to know that she could test positive for COVID-19 based on her symptoms. I knew there was no winning this battle except through prayer. The more afraid I became, the more I prayed. I did not speak of this situation to my husband, any family members, or Pastors. When I received the call, I took God at His Word and ran for shelter under the shadows of His wings; there, I found a hiding place. My daughter and I kept in contact via text messaging. Several days later, my daughter called to tell me that the test she took on July 21st, 2020, showed positive for COVID. I said, what are you going to do? She said, "I will keep working," I said, "what do you mean, keep working?" She said, "momma, I went back to work five days ago,100%!" She had taken the test 2 weeks prior; the results were seriously delayed. During the wait, God had seriously touched her body! Hallelujah!

When the enemy came against me one way, he had to flee seven ways. There were some pretty rough times in 2020 for us, but God kept proving Himself over and over again. It took submitting myself to God; that I could resist the devil, he had to flee. The church buildings closed, but this church, this temple of God, remained open to the will of God for my life. God strengthened me and had Grace and Mercy follow me as we continued to minister Beyond the Altar.

During the 'Safer at Home Mandate,' God provided opportunities for me to connect with other believers via Zoom in other cities and states. For me, that enlarged God in my eyes to assemble with other believers outside of my regular church family gave me strength. We shared testimonies of God's faithfulness. I was moved by the effectual fervent prayers these two groups offered up on behalf of our Pastor at Daystar Family Church, Northport, AL.

Pastor Scott suffered a life-altering event. Through much prayer and God's divine intervention, Pastor Scott's heart was restored to life and love for all people in a deeper way than before. To hear his people pray with such passion was full of strength and joy in the Holy Ghost for me! I want to thank my new niece Stephane Lang for inviting me to join them in Bible Study via Zoom during those difficult times. There was such a newness of life interacting with those two groups each week. I was encouraged simultaneously as God provided plenty of opportunities for me to encourage others in the faithfulness of our mighty God!

During 2020, Though enemies were encamped all around me, I was surrounded by God's love for me, so I raised my hands in surrender to all that God had for me. I leaned on Him even more. Sometimes It felt like I was having an out-of-body experience seeing and hearing the horrible stories of 2020, but God kept me in perfect peace as I kept my mind stayed on Him. Watching God's word unfold in my life was absolutely amazing! Looking to Him for everything was and is an adventure! I became even more determined to take God at His word. I became all the more confident in His faithfulness! He was and continues to be my sustainer, the lifter up of my head, my peace through every 2020 storm. Weathering the storms are dissimilar from previous times, knowing even more that I could trust Him. I gained a new perspective. In my mind, if not now, when! When will we trust Him? When will we take Him at His word? The grandest opportunity was now at our dispense to present the gospel to the world. "To go ye therefore" no longer required a jet. We traveled swiftly via live stream and other technology.

Ministering Beyond the Altar was the catalyst of peace and strength during 2020. As I poured into others, God poured even more into my life. The exchange utterly enhanced my faith walk.

Through the beginning of the SAFER AT HOME MANDATE in 2020, my love for painting was restored. I found peace in painting and listening to instrumental worship, gospel and jazz music. At times classical music calmed the storm also. I remember the days where I would get up before daybreak to worship and pray to the Lord through painting. I would be in the same spot painting when my husband returned home from work late in the evening. Some of my paintings earned enough to transition the ministry into a 501c3 nonprofit organization.

Through prayer and counsel with the Holy Spirit, this decision to widen the efficiency of the ministry into a nonprofit organization during the 2020 pandemic enabled us to enlarge our reach to those in need. We look forward to all that the Lord has in store for us at Beyond the Altar Ministries. For we know where our help comes from. God has been an ever-present help in every area of need. All at the same time. I'm so glad that we don't have to wait until He finishes being healer for one before He can be a way-maker for another. I'm glad that He is able to look after me at the same time He looks after the widow, the single mom, the orphan, and the one in jail. He can feed the hungry while intervening in an angry marital dispute.

I tell you the truth, the Joy of the Lord is my strength, has been my strength, continues to be my strength and everlasting joy! Someone asked, "how did you make it through 2020?" I found a hiding place under the shadow of His wing. I found His strength in the secret place, in the stillness. He was there in the quiet hours where I waited to watch His word unfold.

Many of us viewed the 2020's Pandemic as a weakness for us. On the contrary, it caused many to turn their hearts back to God. It caused His people who are called by His name to humble ourselves and pray. The 2020 Pandemic was the catalyst for a dying generation to turn from their wicked ways. In spite of what it looks like, unity came as we suffered the fear of the deadly Corona Virus globally. The pot could no longer call the kettle black because we all needed God's healing power to touch every nation. In the midst of playing the blame game in politics and dealing with Black Lives Matter and blue lives matter, God said in John 3:16 that ALL LIVES MATTER. I sent my son Jesus for whosoever will. I love all of my creation. I love the Jew and the gentile, the saint and the sinner. Jesus came as a ONCE FOR ALL SACRIFICE. Had He not shed His blood, there would be no remission of sin. Jesus paid our debt. He repealed on our behalf. He bought our pardon. We do not have to wait on Easter Day to celebrate His resurrection from the grave with all power in His hands. He still has the keys to death, hell, and the grave. Because He lives, I can face tomorrow; I know who holds my future. Because He lives, fear is diminished. That does not mean I do not have fear come upon me sometimes; it means I no longer have to walk in fear. I have received the perfect love of God that casts out all fear.

God is real. Yes, God is real. God is sovereign. God is supreme. He holds us in His hands. I cannot explain all the deaths and the sicknesses, but I will continue to magnify Him above every sickness, every disease, every illness, every circumstance issue and concern that I have, or you have. We have made God too small in our eyes, oh! Lord, please forgive us. We have believed in our hearts that He was unable to help us. But now, oh! Lord, we see our wrong. He is mighty in battle. God is for us, not against us. Our sins are against us. The wages of sin is death, but the gift of God is eternal life.

He is El Elyon, The Most High God
He is Adonai, Lord, Master
He is Yahweh, Lord, Jehovah
He is Jehovah Nissi, The Lord My Banner

He is Jehovah Raah, The Lord My Shepherd
He is Jehovah Rapha, The Lord That Heals
He is Jehovah Shammah, The Lord Is Here and There
He is Jehovah Tsidkenu, The Lord Our Righteousness
He is Jehovah Mekoddishkem , The Lord Who Sanctifies You
He is El Olam , The Everlasting God
He is Elohim, God
He is Qanna, Jealous about you
He is Jehovah Jireh, The Lord Will Provide
He is Jehovah Shalom, The Lord Is Peace
He is Jehovah Sabaoth, The Lord of Hosts

I assure you, being asked to give my account of 2020 in Pen It Volume I and II have been a lifter up of my head. For they overcame by the blood of the Lamb and the words of their testimony. In fact, I still have a red scarf over my door as the scripture tells how they were instructed to splash blood over their doors so that the plague would Passover their homes.

Our Exodus is near; God is faithful. His mercy endures forever. There is no love like the love of God. Being in His presence as I write these words on March 19, 2021, is a testimony of His faithfulness. But oh Lord, our Lord, how excellent is your name in all the earth, what is man, that you are mindful of him, the son of man that you would visit him. You've made us a little lower than the angels and crowned me with glory and honor. Oh Lord, I magnify your name! As the Lord continues to give His angels charge over us, let everything that has breath praise the Lord! For He has certainly done great things! Bless His holy name! I will bless the Lord at all times; His praise shall continually be in my mouth. I will tell my soul to bless the Lord and forget not all of His benefits! I will enter into His gates with praise and into His courts with thanksgiving. I will bless His name.

I will give Him the highest praise, HALLELUJAH! He is worthy of praise! Worthy of glory, worthy of Honor! I will say of the Lord, He is my God! I will tell the world wherever I go about His son Jesus and all He has done for me. I will tell the world how the Holy Spirit comforted me during the very hard times of the Pandemic 2020. How? He is my Friend even still in 2021. I will tell the world stories of how we go way back. How? He was faithful towards me even when I was not. He is a faithful God! I know Him as a counselor when I needed someone to just listen. There are no social distance guidelines with Him. The closer I got to Him, the closer He came to me. There is no six-foot rule with Him. I can get face-to-face. I'm POSITIVE that you can do the same. He is no respecter of persons. There's only one color that matters, RED-HIS BLOOD.

I find it interesting that articles written about COVID showed an illustration of a red prickly substance. Each time I saw this, I saw Jesus' blood covering every ounce of me. Oh! The blood of Jesus! There is healing in the blood of Jesus! There is power in the blood. There is joy in the blood. There is peace in the blood. There is deliverance in the blood. Salvation is in the blood! Forgiveness is in the blood. Hope is in the blood of Jesus. "Hope thou in me, says the Lord! Whatever it is that we need is in the blood. He makes all things new. Believe on the Lord Jesus.
I have truly enjoyed writing these words to edify my God and encourage all those that read them. I'm encouraged, and I wrote them! The opportunity to make my boast upon the Lord has made a powerful impact in my life. I hope it does the same for others. I do not desire just to say something; I have something to SAY.

I thank God for the opportunity to take up space in a book with great authors. Those with prolific writing abilities that surely surpass my own, however, I say with all humility that the spirit of the Lord is upon me. He has anointed me to bring good news! News that will set the captive free makes the spiritually blind to see.

~It is my desire for you, that after reading these words, that if you don't remember my name just remember why I came~

Dirt Rubbing Dirt
-G. Jean Wells-

Did you take a bath today?
What did you see?
Did you walk along the way?
Where did you go?

Hurry and do the things you need to do in life before it's too
late.
Because what you saw in the tub and along the way is a
message to know that this sign can offer strife.

For life is but a fleeting moment that rubs the earth each day.
Avoid the strife and cling to the best things in life.

So, when we wash and walk and rub this life form of dirt,
Remember that we are but clay vessels formed on this earth.
And we will all return from whence we came.

When you wash and walk and live this life of strife,
Take the time to think and look at what this life holds dear,
Try to live a life full of love and abundance before we return to
the dust.
For we are mere mortals that are dirt rubbing dirt.

In honor of the late Georgia Mae Burroughs
Greensboro, AL

The Year the Earth Stood Still
-Peachi Williams-

2020. It's supposed to be a good year. Well, it was but no one expected things to turn out the way they did. We've always heard that 2020 would bring something new ... a change that we'd always remember. I'm sure no one will forget it. I won't, and here's why:

In January, I was excited. It's a new year! Time to get things in order, time to make some changes and time to get things right. I'd been excited about the upcoming college fairs and other things I had going on in my businesses. My schedule was booked and busy, I'd gotten some new contracts and every weekend I was set to be off in another state. Things were looking really good. Although there was some talk about this virus that was going on overseas, there wasn't a huge panic here in the states. I watch the news and read everything, so it was definitely on my radar, but people were going about their lives doing what they do best – focusing on themselves. I had a college fair at the end of the month in Maryland where I first introduced the shirts from our new line and almost sold out. I also had lunch and dinner with some colleagues I hadn't seen since the previous year. Good times were on a roll.

Continuing into February, I was like, life was good! I had planned a trip with my girls and we were all meeting in Atlanta. The fabulous four, we've been a crew since ... (none of your business). We always try and take a trip together at least once a year but attend so many events as a collective it's like we're stuck in a time warp. One thing's for certain – it's always good to be around people who love you. I had a college fair one weekend, then hopped in my truck to drive to Atlanta the next. We had a blast doing almost absolutely nothing. Well, we went to the Trap Museum and some other places, but since I've lived there, it wasn't a really big deal to me. All I cared about was being with my girls, having a little down time, and mentally getting ready for yet another plane trip the following week, and that's when everything started going south.

This trip was the very last memory before everything went crazy. We witnessed the death of Ahmaud Arbery as he was basically targeted and gunned down. That took a toll, as I felt that more was to come. There was just something about 2020 that started having an unsettling feeling. I had a gala in Delaware to attend in March but found myself getting the ticket banked for future use. The numbers of people getting this COVID thing was starting to get scary, and it made you start wondering what was really going on. People were getting really sick and starting to die. Things were about to be different.

March was different. Things were getting shut down and people couldn't go out. The stores were starting to run out of everything – food, toilet paper, wipes, Lysol, hand sanitizer. You name it – they didn't have it. I thought a lot about what was going to happen – what we were facing. And then, here we go again. Breonna Taylor was killed while sleeping in her bed. It made me feel as if we were being targeted as a people. I knew things were going to start getting crazy because of the upcoming election later in the year, but this was starting to feel like "game on" with black folks as the main characters. Business wise, I also wondered what that would look like for me, a person whose livelihood depended on my ability to serve my clients. With two brands, things could get crazy. But ... there's a GOD. I was able to secure supplies before everything went bust. I guess because I'm a planner, I saw the writing on the wall. For me, things kept moving and I continued to persevere.

As the year progressed, we went through so much turmoil, but things did have a positive spin in certain aspects. I dug in, kept my existing client list and gained more since everything was being done online. I learned how to pivot in the midst of distress and truthfully, 2020 was a really good year for my businesses. Then, all hell broke loose. May 2020 – we watched

George Floyd senselessly murdered in cold blood on a public street. Who would have ever thought we would be witnessing this in 2020? I will admit, it made my blood boil. I continued to plan, hurting deeply while trying to navigate the pivot and understanding this digital transformation. I met a lot of online colleagues and started realizing certain things that had to be done in order for my business to continue thriving.

I did have some issues – I had to send a brand a cease and desist for using my trademark. Sadly, it was one of us. I really wish people took the time to do the research and not take the stance of using someone else's intellectual property just because they want to. That's one of the biggest things small business owners and entrepreneurs lack – they don't know and don't want to do the work to find out. With so many digital entrepreneurs selling a dream, it's easy to get lost in the fray. Business owners should take what they can apply and the rest, let it go. Don't try and be like someone else just because they claim they've done all these things and made all this money. Truthfully, wealth whispers.

After the George Floyd murder, the entire world was in an uproar. Riots, looting and protests seemingly became the norm. Black Lives Matter in the midst of an undercover outgoing racist president and we're stuck in the middle of it. Shortages on supplies, businesses shutting their doors and the pandemic getting worse by the day. I felt like we lived in a twilight zone. Luckily, I was still being blessed. My Freshman Fun Box partnerships were still paying off and I continued delivering. The caveat – I was able to secure PPE for our boxes for every month of the year. That was a blessing and folks are still wondering how I was able to find these things when no one had them available. I call it GRACE.

Right after the George Floyd killing, big businesses were scrambling to find small businesses they could tap into and donate goods and services. Imagine my surprise when someone from AmproGel called and said they wanted to give us product. We ended up with an entire storage unit of hair products and other items. Can you say blessed? I was still working with my ambassadors on the Freshman Fun Box side, and foundations and other organizations I deal with were still putting through orders even though most students were confined to their homes for their freshman year of college.

On the writing side, business was also very busy for me and all I could do every single day was thank God for allowing me to sustain during these difficult times. It's funny how we don't think about the things that could happen. I always like to think about the positive, but with each passing day, things just seemed to societally get worse. What were we supposed to do? What are we supposed to think? Every day I watched as more people unveiled who they really were, and it was sickening. But, you have to keep a smile on your face and keep it moving, right? I tried to make light of 2020 – I made t-shirts that said, "2020, I need a reset button," and "2020? Nah, I'm good." The crazy part is this is how almost everyone was feeling.

One of the most enlightening things that happened in 2020 was the realization that black people need to remove the blinders. The police are doing exactly what they were trained to do, and that's not on the side of goodness for the black and brown. The farce of a presidential election was embarrassing. It's obvious how things turned out leading up to and after the election that black people are still being minimized no matter how it looks. Yes, it's cool to be black again, or is it? HBCU's are cool again. Or are they? No, not really.

Although we were confined in 2020, a lot of good things happened. People learned how to spend quality time with one another again. I got my braces off, and I hit a milestone – 50 years old. Wow. Although I had planned to have a big shindig, it turned out to be a virtual get together right before Christmas. This was the very first time I spent Thanksgiving, my birthday, Christmas and New Year's alone.

I've realized that as a people we need to become self-sufficient and independent. People should be getting their financial homes in order and figuring out next steps. Moving into 2021, my businesses were having one of the best years in their entire existence, and it clear the strategies I took time to consider throughout 2020 are working. Looking to the future, I see success and a lot of other things on the horizon. I've never really taken things or life for granted, but I do hope others start adopting that mindset as well.

In terms of taking care of your business, I strongly suggest getting your names and things trademarked. I also suggest getting around REAL people that are likeminded. Protect your investment and protect your secrets. Make folks sign NDAs. Make people earn their place in your circle. The business world can be very cutthroat, so it's important to know who you are. Belief in self is key. Your journey is unlike anyone else's, so learn and enjoy it as you go. Don't give up. Eventually, you'll make your mark. If you haven't learned anything else in 2020, it's to take care of YOU.

No one owes you anything, but you DO owe yourself. You owe yourself grace, self-care and confidence in your abilities to move mountains. If you want it bad enough, you'll get there. Stop believing all these people who say they made a million overnight. If you really knew the truth, you'd be shocked. Walk your walk and run when you must but remember – everything must be decent and in order even if everyone else around you are doing something different.

It takes courage to move differently when people question your moves. It also takes determination to keep things moving when you feel like giving up. Know this – you are divinely appointed to do what you were called to do. If you were given a vision, it will make room for you. All you have to do is MOVE on it. Thank you 2020 for showing me what life should and shouldn't be, what I want and don't want, and how I envision the progression of my businesses. Imparting knowledge on others is a gift I never want to lose.

To the ends of the earth ...

CO-AUTHORS
-Contributors-

Pen It
The People's Accounts, Emotions, and Thoughts of 2020

Volume II

Tony Harris Brooks

Tony Orlanda Harris Brooks, is a published author of "STILL" She is also as contributing author in "Pen It, Volume I." Her bio is listed in Marquis Who's Who in the East. She also has published poems with Iliad Press of Big Rapids Michigan and is a life-long member of The National Poetry Society. Tony Orlanda Harris Brooks, formerly known as Tony Harris, recently married Terry Edward Brooks and resides in Cottondale, AL.

She studied nursing at Iona College and business at Shelton State Community College.

Romi Darling

Romi Darling is a licensed makeup artist/Creative Assistant CEO of DolledbyRomi Enhancing the Beauty Within. Her goal is to own a beauty bar and a plus-size model agency.

One of her most recent achievements was completing college in 2020. Additionally, she competed and won the first "Ms. Full Figure Plus Alabama" in 2021. Romi states, "I'm solely here to use my platform "Passion & Purpose."

Contact information Facebook - Romi Darling Instagram- DolledbyRomi

Dr. Dionne Edison

Dr. Dionne Edison is a retired educator with over 45 years of formal service. She has worked with students of all ages from toddlers in family day care homes through higher education. She has published two books: "March of the C.O.W.S: Creatures of Wonderful Simplicity," a short whimsical book of poetry and prose; and "Success Beyond Academics: How to Set Expectations for Life." co-authored with her daughter, Mrs. Asenath Edison-Gay, to help individuals gain the knowledge and the resources needed to assess their skills, maximize their potential, and live a life of purpose. Additionally, she is the co-author of "Pen It Volume I"

Sheila D. Green
Sheila D. Green is a certified Life Coach trained in psychology, counseling and social work. Sheila is a motivational speaker addressing marriage, family relationships and self-care awareness. She has been working in these areas for the past 20 years. She has extensive experience counseling single and married women. She is an experienced Life Coach skilled in helping to improve relationships, improve health and wellness, and helping clients to execute strategies that lead to effective outcomes and positive living. Sheila is the author of the book, "The Business of a Successful Marriage: Treating Your Marriage Like a Business." and co-author of "Pen It Volume I." She was featured in the May issue of Onyx Magazine as a new rising author. Her second book on self-care is coming soon. Sheila is the president and CEO of SDGreen Consulting. In all of Sheila's work, she draws from her experiences of being married for over 32 years and raising two children with her husband Lee. Learn more at sdgreenconsulting.com.

Emma Hall
Emma Hall a mother of two sons, eight grandchildren, a publisher author, song writer, arm bearer, culinary of soothing food for the soul, worshiper, A lover of God and His people. Created to help and encourage women in their God given purpose.

Rev. Dr. B. Nelson Little
B. Nelson Little has Pastored the Galilee Baptist Church in Panola, Alabama, for over 20 yrs. He initiated a progressive ministry to bring hope, help, and healing to the Body of Christ. In 2006 the Church was burned by arson. Pastor Little led the congregation to forgive, and they rebuilt a 10,000 sq ft state-of-the-art facility in Panola, AL. Along with rebuilding, Pastor

Little has helped plant Churches in the Federal Prison in Aliceville, Alabama, a Missional Church in Tishebee, Alabama, and assisted in the building of other Churches in Rural Alabama.

Pastor Little is a native of Panola, Alabama, and educated in the Sumter County school system. He studied at Alabama State University, Faulkner University, Samford University, Lifeway Bible Training, Hamilton, Ashwood, and American Baptist Seminary.

Rev. Dr. Little is also the founder and lead singer for the chart-topping group Rev. Bob Little and the Soulfulairs. Additionally, he is the producer and host of "Faith for Your Future" radio program and serves as President of Sharper Brothers Records, Atlanta, Georgia.

Rev. Dr. Little also serves as Dean of Christian Education for the New Era Progressive Missionary Baptist Convention of Alabama and Vice Moderator of the Northbound Bethlehem District. He is a member of Phi Beta Sigma Fraternity, Kappa Kappa Psi Band Fraternity, Mighty Marching Hornets, and many other civic and fellowship groups. Pastor Little has led his congregation to the first dual Alliance Church in Rural West Alabama and has led the movement for racial reconciliation in the Rural area.

He is married to Barbara Daniel-Little, and the father of Jasmine.

Antorinette Lott
Antorinette Lott is known as Annette and Minister Lott. She has a handsome and wonderful son (Rashad) and a beautiful, energetic daughter (Rachel). In addition, she has been blessed to be called Nana by five wonderful grandchildren. (Zinnia, Sienna, Rayden, Jaceon, and King).

She is an Alabama native; however, the most impactful years of her life were spent in Chicago Heights, IL. She is a proud US Army Veteran and 30 plus years in retail leadership. She is deeply passionate about community involvement; she believes that everyone should contribute to the wellness of their community; working together will assuredly bring safety, success, and beauty to any community.

Her journey to becoming an author has been amazing and intense. Her first book was a healing journey; writing about the fears and pain of her youth gave her the courage to let go and trust God. Writing helped her conquer the battle with MS and has been a great escape during this pandemic.

The love for God and sharing what he gives her has been the most rewarding thing she has done, aside from being blessed with her children. Antorinette states, "I thank God for blessing me with the gift and passion for writing."
Her favorite scripture is,
Be not conformed to this world but be ye transformed by the renewing of your mind, that ye may prove what is that good and acceptable, and perfect, will of God. Romans 12:2

Cheyenne C. Nickelberry
Cheyenne C. Nickelberry is a Christian artist and poet. Additionally, she is a member of Media Ministry Team at Tabernacle Missionary Baptist Church in Detroit, MI. She is a student at Michigan State University.

Her favorite scripture is "But be ye doers of the word and not hearers only, deceiving your own selves" James 1:22

Sharonda Palmer
Sharonda Palmer is a 39-year-old mother of three. She was born and raised in Northport, AL. She's been writing since high school but recently picked back up her pen during this pandemic and got back into journaling.

LaQueisha Price

Laqueisha Price is an entrepreneur and visionary. She currently lives in Tuscaloosa Alabama. A few year ago, something took place in her life that led her to become women she is today, an author, mentor and transformational coach. Laqueisha states, "New things happen in our lives every day! Be sure to follow me on all social media platforms at Laqueisha Price.

Contact information: Laqueishaprince35@gmail. Com or you can go to my websites at https://linktr.ee/MrsAlabama1, www.priceless-service.com, or via email at laqueishaprince35@gmail.com.

Reginald Prince

Reginald Prince is an entrepreneur. He states, "I'm married to a Queen." He is the father of even children. He is also incarcerated at Yazoo Mississippi correctional facility, presently serving a 10-year sentence. During this time, he chose to write and work on his personal development. "I'm grateful for this opportunity," said Reginald. I can be connected by email at laqueishapeince35@gmail.com or Reginald Prince 35969-001 Federal Correctional Complex Yazoo City USP P.O. Box 5000
Yazoo City, MS 39194

Kena Reshay

K. Reshay is a self-published author, poet and playwright. She was a featured panelist and presenter at the 2019 NATIONAL Book Club Conference in Atlanta, GA.

In 2017, her debut book series "Appearances," provoked readers to examine the people amongst their circles.

As the President and Founder of Me Time Book Club, she has participated in several book and community service events throughout the years. The goal of her book club is to promote literacy within the community.

Her latest standalone novel "All Things Work Out Well," depicts the heartbreaking story of tragedy and triumph amongst two friends. In addition, she has released two stage plays and a children's book co-authored with her two sons.

Currently, she is working on her personal travel memoir "African American Girl Lost." This memoir outlines her personal journey of self discovery during her first visit to West Africa.
She resides in Alabama with her husband and two sons.

Kamia Wardlaw
Kamia Wardlaw was born and raised in Detroit, Michigan. She is 19 and has been singing since the age of 5. She comes from a musical family and has always loved learning and listening to Gospel, Soul, and R&B music and singing in the church choir. Her favorite artist includes Mary Mary, The Clark Sisters, Sheléa Frazier, and Tamia.

She graduated from the Detroit School of Arts High school in 2019 as a vocal major, performing Jazz and Classical. Presently, she attends Talladega College, studying Psychology. She performs with the Talladega College Choir and has always had a heart for music and singing.

Cece Washington
Cece Washington is married to Alex Washington since 1990; they met in Alex's northern hometown in 1985. They went down South to start fresh with their four children just a few days after saying "I Do". She unapologetically raves about her eight "nana babies" very often in conversation. A good number of single moms she has ministered to still refer to her as their spiritual mom.

She is the Founder and CEO/Director at Beyond the Altar Ministries, a 22-year-old ministry birthed in 1998; however, just becoming a 501©3 Non-Profit Tax Exempt Organization on July 14, 2020. She is honored to be recognized by her Pastor, Dr. Scott Schatzline, since 2018 as a Para-Mission Minister/ Home Missionary. A missionary in and to her own community, a minister of reconciliation to one "homeless working single mom family" at a time. However, ministering to the needs of all people "Beyond the Altar," she continues to serve as a Pastoral Care Worker at Daystar Family Church in Northport, Alabama. This has been her family's home church since 1993 under the leadership of Dr. Scott Schatzline and founder/spiritual dad, Bishop Patrick Schatzline. Additionally, Cece continues to serve as a chaplain at the local hospitals.

Prior leadership roles include active membership for the Tuscaloosa Salvation Army Women's Auxiliary as Fundraising Coordinator and chaplain for The Good Samaritan Clinic of Tuscaloosa. In addition, for many years, Cece offered spiritual counseling by private referral to many women that visited a local health clinic.

She launched BTA Institute on May 22, 2019, where she now serves as Chancellor while simultaneously studying to receive a Doctorate of Theology. Cece is the proud author of "Tennis Wife," published in 2016 and many other unwritten books, as she often states. She is also the co-author of "Pen It, Volume I." Cece loves to worship, pray and read the word. Hosting Bible Studies brings her much joy. In her free time, Cece loves to paint, create DIY projects and repurpose common-use household items. Most items are given away as she ministers "Beyond the Altar."

Much of the events mentioned above and information took place after she suffered a stroke in 2008, paralyzing her left side. However, Cece continues to "go on to live victoriously," serving God and spreading JOY wherever she goes. She always looks for the light in every dark situation bringing hope to each one she meets, all to the glory of God. Praise ye the Lord! Hallelujah!

Gladys Jean Willis Wells

Gladys Jean Willis Wells was born in Northport, Alabama, in 1954. She attended Matthews Elementary School, Riverside High, Tuscaloosa County High, University of Alabama, and the University of West Alabama, receiving a Bachelor's degree in Home Economics, a Master's degree in Early Childhood, and an Administration Certification.

She is a member of First Baptist Church, Northport, Alabama, NEA (Retired), and Zeta Phi Beta Sorority, Inc. Seasonal crafts and bargain shopping are two of her favorite interests.

Gladys is married to James, and they have two daughters, Nicole and Sharonda. In addition, she is a loving Geegee to seven grandchildren.

Peachi Williams

Peachi Williams is a multifaceted entrepreneur. As the founder and CEO of The Write Mixx, Inc., she runs a creative content and brand engagement firm helping individuals, consultants and businesses connect with their niche audiences. Widely known as "The Word Wizard," Peachi is a published author and editor, has written for major publications such as *Kontrol and Romantic Times Magazine,* and currently hosts two podcasts, Talk Like a Brand and Respectably Raw.

Other ventures include the Brandpreneur Academy, solely dedicated to helping entrepreneurs find their branding niche, and The Freshman Fun Box brand, which includes The Freshman Box, The HBCU Box, Middle and High School boxes, and the lifestyle brand I'm HBCU.

About the Visionary
-Pam Ryans-

Ms. Pamela (Pam) Ryans is a native of York, Alabama; a resident of Lyman, South Carolina; and is an avid author and empowerment speaker who provide her audiences with captivating and powerful life messages. Her illustrious career began at a reflecting point as she struggled to find her identity in the midst of silence.

Ms. Ryans formalized her education through attendance at Stillman College, a Historically Black College. In pursuit of her purpose, she chose to drop her studies during her senior year. Returning to Stillman ten years later, she completed her Bachelor's Degree in Business Administration with a concentration in Marketing. Pam continued her studies and obtained a Master's Degree in Counseling and Psychology from the University of West Alabama.

In the midst of a diverse and vast life, Pam Ryans is the Founder of "1 Vision Empowerment," where she a life coach and publisher. Through "1 Vision Empowerment," she is the Founder of the Stillman College Alumni Authors Book Dedication and founder of the Books and Brews Author's Showcase. She also provides academic and career workshops for students of all ages. Pam provides inspirational ministry encouragement via "Transform Your Mind with Pam Ryans," (text, email, YouTube videos, and on Facebook). Pam dedicated her personal time, as a caregiver to her mother, who battled Stage IV breast cancer until her recent passing. Through her dedication and an intense desire to support other caregivers, Pam began an organization titled "The Daughter of Sarah". Pam hosts an annual event for the organization and provides gifts to caregivers. Additionally, the program advocates the importance of early detection of all illnesses and an awareness of the family history.

Pam pens her life's journey and is a bestselling author. Unselfishly, Pam is also publisher of other #1 bestselling authors.

Most proudly, Pam mothers four amazing young ladies and is the grandmother of four joys of her life. Her interest is expressing love through knowledge, correction, and expression. She enjoys cooking, music, reading, and just laughing at and with herself and friends.

Her books and services are available at
www.1visionempowerment.com

www.ingramcontent.com/pod-product-compliance
Lightning Source LLC
Chambersburg PA
CBHW072211090426
42740CB00012B/2478